# CONTE

T0030212

# INTRODUCTION

**P**icture yourself in a small boat on a lake during a sunny summer day. The motor is off, the water gently laps at the boat, and a flock of Canada geese honks overhead. You've got all the gear you need, including a fresh bucket of nightcrawlers. Your fishing line buzzes as the lure flies out over the gentle water and lands with a "plunk." It's time to fish for bass!

Bass fishing is both an amazing sport and a relaxing pastime that can be done almost any time of the year. Many bass fishers like to compete against others using the latest technology and methods. Every year, bass fishers meet at tournaments all over the United States and Canada. These take place in rivers, in lakes, and in salt water. It's a rush to hook a bass and haul it in, hoping to land the biggest or heaviest fish in the competition.

Other anglers prefer the peace and quiet of fishing as a hobby. It's not a good idea to go fishing alone, but it can be enjoyable to take a friend or two to the lake for a peaceful afternoon of bass fishing. Many people like to catch, clean, and eat their own bass! Still others enjoy a catch-and-release process, which allows people to enjoy the recreational activity without killing the fish.

There are several kinds of bass, and they live in different environments. Striped bass live in ocean waters near coasts. Largemouth and small-mouth bass can be found in lakes, ponds, rivers,

# THE INSIDER'S GUIDE TO FISHING

# BASS FISHING

## LIKE A PRO

DWAYNE HICKS

ROSEN
PUBLISHING

Published in 2024 by The Rosen Publishing Group, Inc.
2544 Clinton Street, Buffalo, NY 14224

Portions of this work were originally authored by Simone Payment and published as *Bass Fishing*. All new material in this edition was authored by Dwayne Hicks.

Editor: Greg Roza
Designer: Michael Flynn

**Library of Congress Cataloging-in-Publication Data**

Names: Hicks, Dwayne, author.
Title: Bass fishing like a pro / Dwayne Hicks.
Description: [Buffalo] : Rosen Publishing, [2024] | Series: The insider's
    guide to fishing | Includes index.
Identifiers: LCCN 2023030333 (print) | LCCN 2023030334 (ebook) | ISBN
    9781499475920 (library binding) | ISBN 9781499475913 (paperback) | ISBN
    9781499475937 (ebook)
Subjects: LCSH: Bass fishing--Juvenile literature. | Basses
    (Fish)--Juvenile literature.
Classification: LCC SH681 .H55 2024  (print) | LCC SH681  (ebook) | DDC
    799.17/73--dc23/eng/20230711
LC record available at https://lccn.loc.gov/2023030333
LC ebook record available at https://lccn.loc.gov/2023030334

Some of the images in this book illustrate individuals who are models. The depictions do not imply actual situations or events.

*Manufactured in the United States of America*

CPSIA Compliance Information: Batch #CWRYA24. For further information, contact Rosen Publishing at 1-800-237-9932.

and streams. Less common species of bass include spotted bass, white bass, black bass, and white perch. Some bass can only be found in certain areas. In 2013, a new type of black bass, the Choctaw bass, was discovered in creeks and rivers in the Florida Panhandle and southern Georgia.

Bass fishing can be an engaging hobby, but it's a hobby that comes with responsibility. Our natural world has gone through changes, many because of the actions of people. Fish populations are in decline around the world due to pollution and overfishing. Conscientious anglers are careful with the environment and its many living creatures. This is the only way to ensure that fish populations remain plentiful for future generations.

Now let's grab our tackle boxes and all the bait we can carry—let's go bass fishing!

# CHAPTER 1

# LET'S GET STARTED!

F ishing may seem easy to some. Just cast a line and wait for a bite. But there's a lot that goes into becoming a true pro at fishing for any type of fish. Before deciding which type of pole to buy or what kind of bait to use, it's a good idea to spend some time learning about the fish themselves! This knowledge can help you find the best places to fish, the best time of day to fish, and the best baits or lures to use. This knowledge will save you time and frustration in the long run.

## A CLOSER LOOK AT FISH

Fish are vertebrates, which means they have a backbone (vertebrae). Fish are cold-blooded animals. Their body temperature adjusts to match the temperature of the air around them. Fish breathe through flaps of skin on either side of their head called gills. Fish must move through the water for the gills to work. As water flows through the gills, they absorb oxygen from the water.

A fish's fins and muscles power it through water. Scales protect the body, and a coating of mucus over the scales offers defense against infection. The mucus coating also allows fish to move through water quickly.

To help them find food, fish have well-developed senses. They have excellent senses of smell and hearing. Most fish can see in many directions because their eyes are near the top of their head. They can taste with their mouth and tongue but also with the exterior of their body. Fish can also sense food via vibrations in the water.

## BASS OF THE WORLD

The many types of bass can seem rather different from each other. Some bass live in fresh water and others live

As water passes through a fish's gills, very small blood vessels called capillaries allow oxygen that is dissolved in the water to pass into the fish's body. This is how fish breathe.

in salt water. The two major types of freshwater bass are largemouth and smallmouth. Other bass that live in fresh water are spotted bass, white bass, and white perch. Striped bass begin their lives in fresh water, but as adults they spend most of their time in salt water.

Bass are often sorted into two main categories. The larger category are known as black bass. These include largemouth and smallmouth bass but also includes several other species, such as the Choctaw bass and the spotted bass. Temperate bass are different from black bass in several ways, including body size and mouth size. Temperate bass include striped bass, white bass, and white perch.

## LARGEMOUTH BASS

Largemouth bass, the largest type of bass, are a very popular North American fish, partly because they put up a good fight. This can make them a challenge to catch! Light green or brown on top, largemouth bass have a white stomach with dark spots shaped like diamonds on their sides. Largemouth bass are usually between 5 and 10 pounds (2.3 and 4.5 kg) when full grown but can weigh as much as 20 pounds (9 kg).

LARGEMOUTH BASS

## SMALLMOUTH BASS

Smallmouth bass are the second-largest type of bass. They are usually a bit thinner and smaller than largemouth bass, and as the name suggests, they have a smaller mouth. Like the largemouth, they put up a good fight while being caught. Smallmouth bass are brown, gold, or olive green. They are lighter on their sides and have a white belly. Unlike the largemouth, smallmouth bass have red eyes. Smallmouth bass can weigh from 2 to 6 pounds (1 to 2.7 kg) when full grown.

SMALLMOUTH BASS

## OTHER FRESHWATER BASS

Largemouth and smallmouth bass are the most common bass, but there are several other types of freshwater bass. The spotted bass looks similar to the largemouth bass, and the two are often confused. However, spotted bass are smaller. Other ways to tell them apart are that spotted bass have teeth on their tongue and a large spot near their gills.

White bass are good fish for eating. They also put up a good fight! They are usually silver with a dark gray or green back. They have yellow eyes and several dark stripes that run along their sides.

Despite their name, white perch are bass. Like white bass, they are very good for eating. White perch look similar to white bass but have a thin body. They can be olive, grayish green, brown, or even black on their back, with light green or white on their belly. Although most white perch live in fresh water, they can also live in salt water or brackish water. White perch are most common in the five Great Lakes and in rivers along the eastern coast of the United States.

## STRIPED BASS

Striped bass are bluish black or dark green on top with a silver or white belly. Black stripes run along their sides. They have large, long bodies.

Striped bass live most of their lives in salt water. As adults, they live in ocean waters along coasts. When female striped bass are ready to lay eggs, they swim up freshwater rivers connected to the ocean. After they lay their eggs, they swim back out to the ocean. Many of the eggs are food for predators, particularly other fish. The young fish, known as hatchlings, spend their early lives in the river. In time, the young striped bass swim out to the ocean.

Some striped bass live only in fresh water. Some of these freshwater striped bass were moved by people to inland freshwater lakes and rivers. Remarkably, they survived and flourished in their new locations. Other freshwater striped bass populations began when the Santee and Cooper Rivers in South Carolina were dammed in the 1940s. Striped bass that had traveled up the rivers to lay eggs became trapped in the reservoirs created by the dams. These bass adapted to the new conditions.

Most striped bass spend the summer in northern waters where it is cooler. They swim farther south, where the waters are warmer, for the fall, winter, and spring.

## BASS FISHING LOCATIONS

Before packing up your gear and heading out, make sure to check fishing regulations in your area. Fishing is prohibited in some places, and some bodies of water are off limits. There can also be restrictions based on the season, so a fishing area may be open some times but not others.

A great way to locate a good fishing spot is to ask a local angler. They will be able to point out not only a good body of water but possibly even the best spot on that body of water. To find a local angler, talk to friends or family, or ask at a bait shop or store that sells fishing gear.

When you find a good fishing spot, make a note of its location. Also note what time the fish were biting, the weather conditions, and the bait used. This information will help when planning future fishing trips.

Workers and owners of local bait shops can help you select the right gear for a fishing trip. They also often know the best places for catching bass.

## WHERE TO FIND LARGEMOUTH

Largemouth bass can be found in many types of bodies of water throughout the mainland United States and a few southern areas of Canada. They can be found in small creeks and ponds, but more often they live in rivers, large ponds, and lakes. They prefer water at about 70°Fahrenheit (21°Celsius) or warmer.

Largemouth bass occasionally look for food near the surface of the water. However, they usually stay well below the surface of the water. They especially like darker water, so they are often found in shady areas, such as below branches or trees that have fallen into the water. They can also be found near low-hanging branches or underneath lily pads. However, largemouth bass will usually only be found in these areas if the water is a few feet deep or more.

## WHERE TO FIND SMALLMOUTH

Smallmouth bass prefer clearer water than largemouth bass. They are most often found in streams and clear lakes with rocky bottoms. They are also happier in cooler water than largemouth bass—about 65°F (18°C). Smallmouth bass can be found throughout most of the United States. They are also widely found in Canada.

## WHERE TO FIND OTHER FRESHWATER BASS

Spotted bass live most often in streams. White bass live in large lakes or rivers. White perch can be found in salt water near the shore and coastal rivers or freshwater lakes and ponds. White perch like to be close to the bottom of any body of water.

Smallmouth bass live in calmer streams and clear lakes. Fishing for them can be a relaxing experience.

## WHERE TO FIND STRIPED BASS

Striped bass that live in salt water usually stay near the shore. They like to look for food around bridges, docks, piers, and rocks. Striped bass spend most of their time looking for food around these structures and near the bottom, but they will come to the ocean surface if they are chasing food. Striped bass move to freshwater streams to lay eggs. At that time, they are usually spotted in the open water in the middle of a river.

The largest populations of striped bass are along the East Coast of the United States. However, there are smaller populations along the Gulf Coast and in the Pacific Ocean off the coast of the northern United States and southern edge of Canada.

Fish that move from salt water to fresh water to spawn and lay their eggs, such as these striped bass, are known as anadromous fish.

## MIGRATION BY TRAIN?

It's not uncommon for striped bass to migrate. They travel from salty coastal waters up freshwater streams to lay eggs. After, they travel back to ocean waters.

Striped bass were introduced to the West Coast of North America during an unusual migration. They were originally brought by train from New Jersey to San Francisco, California, in 1879! While only 132 fish survived the long train trip, 300 more were brought a few years later. Eventually, there was a thriving population of striped bass along the coasts of northern California, Oregon, and British Columbia, Canada. There are not as many now because the coastal rivers where females used to lay their eggs have been dammed to irrigate local crops.

## KINDS OF BAIT

Bass anglers use two types of bait. Many prefer live bait. Small fish, insects, or other things that a fish would eat in its natural environment are examples of live bait. Live bait can be purchased from a bait or fishing shop or can be caught. Other bass fishers prefer lures. Lures are artificial, but they are made to look somewhat similar to natural bait. Bait shops and local anglers can offer good advice on what kind of live bait or lures to use. Some people even make their own lures.

### LIVE BAIT

Worms, crickets, grasshoppers, crayfish, and minnows are all examples of live bait. It can be found at bait shops and

Large earthworms commonly called nightcrawlers are one of the most popular kinds of live bait. They can be found in large amounts in lawns, gardens, backyards, and forests. Many bait stores sell them as well.

sometimes at fishing shops or other local stores. In some areas, bait can even be purchased from vending machines.

Bait can also be collected easily in most areas. You can find worms in nearly any yard, especially after a rain or at night. To keep worms alive and healthy until it is time to fish, make sure they are cool and damp. You can keep them in a small container with air holes. Fill the container with soil, moss, or damp newspaper.

You can use a small net to catch crickets and grasshoppers. They are commonly found in tall grass and wooded areas. Keep insects cool and dry with some grass or dry newspaper in a container with plenty of air holes. Crayfish can be caught with a net in shallow water near rocks. Minnows can also be caught in shallow water with a small net or minnow trap. Store crayfish or minnows in a container with water and air holes until you are ready to use them.

When using live bait, put it on the fishing hook in a way that won't kill the bait. This way, it will still move in the water and attract fish. At the first hint of a nibble on the line when using live bait, tighten the line to "set the hook" in the fish's mouth. Waiting too long could allow the fish to swallow the bait.

## LURES

Lures are artificial forms of bait that are created to look like different live animals that bass like to eat. They can be made of several types of material. Some are made of silvery, shiny metal to look like minnows flashing through the water. Some look like worms, frogs, or other animals. There is also a type of artificial bait that mimics insects. These are called flies. These are made of thread and other fiber. Lures and flies can be purchased at local bait or fishing stores or online. Some people enjoy making their own flies. When using lures and flies, quickly set the hook at the first bite from the fish. Otherwise, the fish may realize that the lure is artificial and lose interest.

## BAIT FOR FRESHWATER BASS

Largemouth bass eat a wide variety of food. They most often eat smaller fish and crayfish. They will also eat frogs, mice, salamanders, snakes, and worms. This means many types of bait are successful at luring in bass. Live bait like minnows and crayfish will attract largemouth bass, but lures will usually work as well.

Smallmouth bass commonly eat smaller fish and crayfish, but they will also eat worms, ants, grasshoppers, ladybugs, leeches, and snakes. Like largemouth bass, smallmouth bass can be caught with live bait or lures.

A spotted bass's favorite meal is crayfish. They will also eat insects, minnows, frogs, worms, and small fish. White bass eat smaller fish and a variety of insects and crayfish. White perch eat small fish, crabs, and shrimp.

## BAIT FOR STRIPED BASS

Striped bass will eat smaller fish, squid, worms, and crabs—they're not picky eaters! They are happy to eat live bait but will eat dead bait too. Although eels and clams aren't what they usually eat, chopped eels and clams can be used to attract striped bass.

## THE BEST TIMES TO FISH FOR BASS

The best time to fish varies by location. Asking local anglers when they have had luck can be helpful. Many fishing websites provide useful information about where and when to find bass. Some state and local environmental agencies post local fishing information on their websites.

In general, the cooler weather of spring and fall is best for freshwater bass, but bass can also be caught in the summer. In some southern locations, bass can be caught in the winter months as well.

Overcast days usually make for ideal fishing weather. Another good time is just before it rains. However, it's not usually good to fish after rain or when it is windy, because the water is stirred up too much. Most bass prefer to feed when the water is clearer. Early to mid-morning is usually the best time of day to fish. The last few hours before sunset can also be a good time to locate bass.

In the hours just before dark, bass are usually more active. Fishing during this time is also a great way to enjoy a beautiful sunset.

## RECORD BREAKERS!

There is a tie for the largest largemouth bass ever landed. On June 2, 1932—many years before bass world records were recorded—a man named George Perry was fishing on Lake Montgomery in Georgia to find food for his family. Perry caught a largemouth bass that weighed 22 pounds and 4 ounces (10.09 kg)! This fish did indeed feed his family—for two days! Perry soon heard of a fishing contest held by *Field & Stream* magazine. He couldn't send a photo of the fish, but fortunately he had the fish weighed at a local post office. The results were certified soon after. In addition, Perry's family provided the only known photograph of the record-breaking fish in 2006. Perry has held this record for more than 90 years!

In 2009, a man in Japan named Manabu Kurita was fishing in Japan's largest freshwater lake, Lake Biwa. Kurita pulled in a largemouth bass that weighed 22 pounds and 5 ounces (10.1 kg)! This is one ounce (28.3 grams) heavier than the bass that Perry landed in 1932. The International Game Fish Association (IGFA), which began recording record-break- ing catches around 1948, confirmed the weight of Kurita's catch but declared it a tie with Perry's. This is because its rules say that a fish needs to beat the previous record by at least two ounces (56.7 g).

Today, the IGFA recognizes both Perry and Kurita as the official record holders for the largest largemouth bass ever caught.

# CHAPTER 2

# FISHING GEAR

**A**s with other sporting hobbies, bass fishing can become costly. Companies offer a very large range of fishing gear, from simple weights and bobbers to new, high-tech sonar equipment and flashy boats. While there are tons of extras that could be purchased, many items are unnecessary to become a successful bass fisher. Fishing requires very little specialized clothing or safety equipment. There are a few things any angler will need, though. A pole, fishing line, hook, and bait are the basic required items.

## RODS AND REELS

A fishing pole can be as simple as a wood rod with a fishing line and hook attached to the end of it. The first fishing poles were likely tree branches or pieces of bamboo. A pole is easy to make, or one can be purchased. Because there is no reel to control the fishing line, with a pole an angler flicks the line into the water. When a fish bites, simply pull the fish out of the water.

Most rods are made to have a spot to attach a reel of fishing line. Round metal guides run the length of the rod to keep the line in place. Modern fishing rods are usually made of a flexible material called fiberglass.

Fishing line is usually made of nylon and is a single strand (called a monofilament). Most fishing line is clear, but it also comes in other colors including red, blue, green, and yellow. There are different strengths of fishing line, and each strength can hold up to a certain amount of weight. The packaging will tell how many pounds (or kilograms) a particular line can hold.

There are several types of reels to hold fishing line. Each is used for a different purpose, such as big-game fishing or fly fishing. Spin-casting reels are the easiest to

There are several different kinds of reels used in fishing, depending on the fisher's level of skill and the fish they are hunting for. Some reels are more complex than others.

use. They attach to a fiberglass rod, and the fishing line is enclosed within the reel. Spin-casting reels sit on top of the fishing rod.

Spinning reels take a little more practice to use because the fishing line is not enclosed in a spinning reel. This means it can get tangled, which can ruin a day of fishing. The advantage to a spinning reel is that it is possible to cast farther out into the water. They attach to fiberglass or graphite rods and sit on the underside of the rod.

Professional bass anglers often use bait-casting reels. The reel winds the line from side to side, not around in a circle. The advantage of using a bait-casting reel is that an angler can be more specific about when to release the line. However, the fishing line can easily get tangled, making this

This is a bait-casting reel, also called a bait caster.

type of reel difficult to use. Bait-casting reels are used on fiberglass or graphite rods and attach to the top of the rod.

## HOOKS AND LURES

Another essential piece of equipment is the hook. Anglers usually keep a bunch of hooks in their tackle box. Hooks can sometimes get lost when fishing line breaks or when a fish manages to take off with one.

There are two types of hooks: single and treble. Single hooks, which are used for bait, have just one hook. Treble hooks have three hooks and are most often used with lures. Some lures feature more than three hooks. These are often used for larger fish.

## COMMON LURES

| lure name | description | used for |
|---|---|---|
| CRANKBAIT, PLUG | small, plastic, light, colored to look like prey fish | casting, trolling |
| JIG | heavy weight on one end, a hook on the other, various body shapes | casting, vertical fishing, ice fishing |
| SPINNERBAIT | hook on one end, metal blade that spins in the water to reflect light | casting, trolling |
| SPOON | metal, curved so it wobbles while moving through the water, reflects light | casting, trolling, ice fishing |
| CHATTERBAIT | similar to a jig, includes a metal blade that wobbles while moving through the water, plastic frills | casting, trolling |
| TOPWATER | hollow and light so it floats, colored to look like prey fish | casting |
| FLY | a single hook decorated to look like insect prey | fly fishing, casting |

Hooks are sold with and without barbs, which are sharp points at the tip of the hook. It is best to buy barbless hooks because they cause much less damage to the fish. If barbless hooks are not available, you can carefully file the barbs off the hook with a metal file. Or you can bend the barb "closed" using pliers.

Hooks and lures are sharp! They need to be to quickly snag a curious fish. Always handle hooks with care. Wearing gloves may help, but sharp barbs can go through most glove material. Always be careful when casting to avoid "hooking" yourself or others.

## OTHER BASIC EQUIPMENT

Rods, reels, hooks, and bait are all necessary supplies. You may be able to borrow these from a friend or family member. You can also find used equipment at sporting goods stores or online. Always keep in mind that fishing equipment can be sharp and dangerous. Always handle your tackle box and its contents with care.

In addition to the gear an angler will absolutely need to have, there's other equipment that will make fishing easier, and perhaps more enjoyable. Snap swivels are clips that attach to the end of the fishing line. Swivels allow anglers to easily put hooks or lures on the line without having to cut the line or tie new knots each time. Snap swivels move around freely so that the fishing line does not become twisted when hooks and lures move through the water.

Anglers use weights called sinkers, attached to the fishing line above the hook, to help the hook sink to the bottom. Bobbers, on the other hand, keep part of the line afloat so that the hook does not sink too deeply. Bobbers

Tackle boxes often come with numerous compartments and trays to help keep your fishing equipment and tools organized and free from damage. They also help avoid injuries that occur due to haphazard practices.

also bob up and down on the water's surface when a fish takes a nibble of the bait. This alerts the person fishing to pull up on the line to set the fish on the hook.

Tackle boxes are used to store small and sharp equipment—hooks, lures, sinkers, snap swivels, bobbers, and so on. Tackle boxes can be especially handy when using lures. They keep lures separated and can prevent hooks from getting tangled. Tackle boxes are available in stores, but it's also possible to make one out of a box with an egg carton inside it. You can insert your loose hooks in a square of Styrofoam to avoid injuries when reaching for something in your tackle box.

A sharp knife or a pair of scissors is helpful for cutting bait or line. Long-nose or needle-nose pliers are helpful when dealing with hooks and other sharp things. Gloves are also very helpful. Cotton gloves that can be dipped in water are good for handling fish when removing hooks. Thicker gloves can be worn when cleaning fish in preparation for eating.

Some fishers use nets to lift fish out of the water. However, nets can cause a lot of damage to fish. If a net must be used, plastic nets are the best type. These cause much less damage to the fish's protective mucus coating.

## STAYING SAFE

Waders are high, waterproof boots that cover everything below the waist. They are worn when an angler will be standing in a stream or a lake to fish. They keep an angler dry and can offer some protection from the cold. They can also make it easier to walk on a slippery or muddy stream bottom.

## CRAFTING FISHING GEAR

It isn't absolutely necessary to buy equipment in a store. The first fishing gear was made from the resources of the natural world. The oldest tool used for fishing is the spear, made from a simple tree branch. Historians believe that people first started spear fishing about 40,000 years ago!

With a little time and creativity, it's possible to make some basic fishing gear from materials found in a backyard or local woods. A straight tree branch can be turned into a fishing pole. Willow and bamboo are the best woods for a fishing pole because they can bend without breaking. Fibers from dead trees or palm leaves can be woven together to create fishing line. The best trees from which to get fibers are willow, oak, or basswood.

Hooks can be made from numerous objects, including thorns, sharpened wood, or an opened safety pin. A small piece of bark or wood tied to the fishing line a few feet above the hook makes a good bobber. Small pebbles can be used as sinkers. Grubs or beetles for bait can be gathered from rotting logs, worms can be found underground, and crickets can be caught in tall grass.

Always research what the weather will be like where you will be fishing and take the proper precautions. Taking rain gear or a warm jacket on a fishing expedition is always a good idea, even when rain is not expected. Rain can arrive unexpectedly, and weather conditions can change quickly on the open water of a large lake or the ocean. For sunny days, be sure to bring sunglasses, sunscreen, and extra water. Some people also enjoy ice fishing or fishing when it's snowing. Be prepared to stay warm!

Fly fishers often use waders to stay dry and warm when fishing in streams and rivers. Bass fishers have been known to use them when fishing in rivers as well.

One of the most important pieces of safety equipment any angler should have is a personal flotation device (PFD), or life preserver. Anglers should always wear one in a boat or while wading in a stream or river. Even good swimmers should wear a PFD.

On every fishing trip, no matter how big or small, it's important to bring a basic first-aid kit that includes bandages, antibacterial ointment, gauze, and other items to help if an injury occurs. Many common injuries involve accidents with hooks. Always be careful when handling them, and be aware of the people around you when casting.

## ANYTHING ELSE?

You don't need a boat to fish for most types of bass. Bass are often easily caught from the shore, a dock, or a riverbank. Still, many anglers fish from canoes, rowboats, or small engine-powered boats. Some boats are specifically designed for bass fishing. These are most often used by professional bass anglers or other serious anglers. Bass fishing boats are usually very fast. They usually have a fairly flat bottom and are made of fiberglass. The flat bottom allows the boat to go faster and get close to shore in shallow areas. Bass boats have low, flat deck areas in the front and back to make it easy to fish on all sides of the boat. Flat decks also allow anglers to fish standing up.

Bass boats usually have a lot of storage space below the deck. Some are equipped with sonar and GPS. Sonar is also called a depth finder, fish finder, or depth sounder. It shows the underwater environment on a video screen, allowing anglers to see the bottom of the body of water. This includes large objects, such as rocks or coral reefs, as well as schools of fish.

GPS, short for "global positioning system," is a navigational system. GPS devices used for fishing are the same devices that are used in cars. A GPS can help find a specific fishing area if coordinates are already known. Another good use of GPS is "marking" a productive fishing spot. Recording the fishing spot's coordinates will make it easy to find on the next fishing trip. Some GPS systems are so small and portable that they can be used even on rowboats or canoes. You may even have a GPS app on your smartphone!

Not everyone can afford expensive equipment like a GPS and sonar. However, you may be able to rent them from a local fishing business or borrow them from a friend. Many people set out on a fishing trip without these tools.

## CHECK IT OUT

You definitely don't need the newest or most expensive fishing gear to start fishing for bass. You could catch them with a rod, line, and hook! But a fishing trip requires more preparation than that. Consider the following when you are planning a fishing trip, whether it's for the afternoon or for the weekend. You may or may not need all these items, but it's a good idea to plan ahead.

## LIST OF SUPPLIES

- fishing rod and reel
- tackle box to carry everything
- fishing line
- hooks
- lures
- live bait
- bobbers
- sinkers
- gloves
- scissors
- pocketknife
- pliers
- net
- first-aid kit
- fishing license
- map of area
- hat with brim
- waterproof boots/waders
- clothes appropriate to the weather
- snacks/lunch
- drinking water/ice
- radio
- flashlight and batteries
- umbrella
- sunglasses and sunscreen
- insect repellant
- life jackets (PFD)
- cell phone

# CHAPTER 3
# CONSERVATION, SPORTSMANSHIP, AND SAFETY

People go fishing for several reasons. Some love to be outside enjoying nature. Some love to compete in fishing tournaments. Others enjoy spending time with friends and family on a sunny summer day. Regardless of the reason people like to fish, all fishers need to remember three important concepts: respect for the environment, a sense of sportsmanship, and safety.

Respect for the natural world should be a fisher's top priority. Catch-and-release fishing is one very effective way of practicing conservation. Staying safe on the water is another important goal.

Fishing tournaments are popular around the world. Some fishers can make a living taking part in them!

There will be times when you will meet other people fishing in the same area as you. It's always important to be kind to each other and not argue about whose "spot" it is. Don't make tons of noise around others who are fishing. Be careful not to hit anyone with your casts. These are all ways of practicing good sportsmanship.

In bass-fishing tournaments, respect for others and fairness are key to everyone having a good time. Cheating, such as adding extra weights to caught fish, has happened at tournaments. This is unfair to others and a sign of bad sportsmanship. Cheaters who are caught will be banned from future competitions. Some could even face fines and jail time.

## THE BASS TOURNAMENT CHEATING RING

In the early 1980s, a group of men, led by a man from Louisiana named Elro McNeil, were found guilty of cheating at bass-fishing tournaments. Altogether, the group scammed tournaments from Texas to Florida out of approximately $350,000!

McNeil started the scam by purchasing large, frozen black bass, which he thawed out before sneaking them into the tournament. He also provided the other men with their own frozen bass. Altogether, the cheaters "won" seven bass championships.

In April 1985, McNeil was sentenced to five years in prison and fined $5,000. Another man received a similar sentence. Two others were sent to prison for half a year. This story shows that cheating is an unsportsmanlike behavior that won't be tolerated by the people who love the sport of bass fishing. Unfortunately, this is not the last time someone tried to scam a fishing tournament.

If every fisher practices good sportsmanship and conservation practices, fishing can continue to be an enjoyable activity for everyone for many years to come. Poor sportsmanship and irresponsibility can damage the environment, lower fish populations, and, eventually, create fewer opportunities to fish.

Make sure you know local rules and be aware of the surroundings. This includes staying off private property such as land, docks, and beaches. Don't get too close to other anglers when fishing from shore. In a boat, don't get too close to docks, the shore, wading anglers, or other boats. Using common sense should be first and foremost, and "think before acting" is a good rule of thumb.

Anglers need to help take care of the natural environment. This is another example of good sportsmanship. At the end of a day of fishing, it's essential to bring all hooks, fishing line, bait containers, and other garbage home to dispose of or recycle it properly. Collecting hooks and fishing line is especially important. Fish, shorebirds, and aquatic creatures like turtles or salamanders can become tangled in fishing line. Some may try to eat discarded hooks, which can kill them or prevent them from eating food. People can step on misplaced hooks or trip over discarded fishing line. Another way to protect the environment is to only clean fish at home or in specific fish-cleaning stations provided on some docks and marinas. Don't clean fish on a public dock or even along the shore.

Practicing good sportsmanship also means being ethical. This refers to what a person thinks is right and wrong. This is sometimes different from following laws. Just because there's no specific law against something doesn't necessarily mean it's right to do it. Most fishermen consider it unethical to keep fish that are laying eggs. This is

Never throw garbage into the water or on the ground when fishing. This is pollution, and it's also illegal in most fishing locations. If a trash can is not available on-site, bring trash home and dispose of or recycle it.

because it interferes with egg laying and eventually lowers the population of fish. In most states, this is not illegal. But in some locations, waters where fish are known to lay eggs are closed to fishing during the spring.

Catching too many fish is also considered unethical, even if a particular angler has kept only the limit allowed. If every angler keeps the limit on every fishing trip, it could be harmful to the long-term survival of the fish population. Taking small or young fish may be considered unsportsmanlike as well. This can also reduce fish populations.

Returning young fish to the water benefits the fish population, but it also ensures fish populations will be around for future fishers.

## CATCH-AND-RELEASE FISHING

Although there are plenty of people who keep the bass they catch for food, many bass fishers simply enjoy the process of fishing itself. For them, it's not necessary to keep the fish they catch. Instead, they prefer to release fish back into their environment. This practice is known as catch-and-release fishing. This allows the fish to survive and reproduce, resulting in a stronger fish population. Not all fish survive when released, but giving the fish a chance to live is better than not. Good catch-and-release practices can give a fish a better chance of survival.

### THE RULES

Official catch-and-release rules vary by type of fish or even by the body of water. For example, anglers might be allowed to keep a fish of a certain length from one lake, but not a fish of the same length from a lake a mile or two away. This is because environmental officials often make policies based on the fish population in a particular location.

Some fishers have their own unofficial rules about when to keep or not keep a fish. Some always release fish after catching them. Some keep only a certain number per month or year. Some anglers will throw fish that are rare back into the water. Still others always return particularly big fish to the water. Larger, older fish are better able to breed and increase the fish population. Some anglers make the decision to catch and release big fish out of respect for the fish and its ability to survive and reach a large, healthy size.

## CHANCES OF SURVIVAL

Many fish survive after being caught and released back to the water. Just the stress of being caught or handled, however, can cause fish to die. Some factors, or a combination of factors, can make it more likely that fish will die. By avoiding the following things, fishers can increase a fish's chances of survival.

First, an injury to a fish's gills, even a minor one, is something anglers should try to avoid. Keeping the fish out of the water for as short a time as possible is also essential. Most fish can live for about 10 to 20 minutes out of water. The mucus on a bass's body helps keep it alive, but if the mucus is disturbed or wiped off, the fish may die sooner.

A long fight can cause a substance called lactic acid to build up in a fish. This makes it difficult for the fish to process oxygen. Because of this, it's always a good practice to bring the fish to the surface with a minimum of fighting time, if and when that's possible.

The kind of bait used can also affect a fish's chances of survival. Live bait is usually worse for fish because they swallow it more deeply and the hook then causes more internal damage. Where a fish is hooked also makes a difference in its survival. Fish hooked in the mouth, jaw, or cheek generally have the best chances. Fish hooked in the eye or gills usually have a decreased chance of survival due to the damage caused to those body parts.

## SUCCESSFUL PRACTICES

Anglers can do a lot to increase a fish's chance of survival after being released. If possible, keep bass in the water when removing the hook. A good rule of thumb is that fish should not be out of the water longer than 20 seconds at

Bass don't always want to cooperate. It can be difficult to bring them in gently, and they can become injured. Some anglers like this because it's more difficult, and sporting, to land the fish.

a time. This is probably easiest when fishing from shore rather than on a boat. But even on a boat, it is possible to leave the fish in the water when removing a hook.

Compared to other fish, bass usually put up a strong fight when being caught. However, it's usually easier to handle them afterward because they don't wiggle around too much. Keep the fish still by gently holding its tail or, preferably, its jaw—just remember to avoid touching a fish's delicate gills. If possible, anglers can work in teams with one angler holding the fish and the other removing the hook.

This largemouth bass was hooked through its lip. This should make the hook and lure easy to remove. Removal can be difficult or even impossible if a fish swallows a hook.

Most of the time, hooks usually do not go in too deeply in bass, so they are fairly easy to remove. Using barbless hooks makes this process even easier and safer for the fish. To remove the hook, use a pair of long-nosed or needle-nosed pliers to gently ease the hook out of the fish's mouth. It is sometimes possible to simply put some slack in the fishing line for the hook to come right out. If the hook does not come out right away using pliers or slack in the line, don't tug or pull hard. This can rip the fish's mouth or gills.

When a fish becomes deeply hooked, some experts recommend cutting the line and leaving the hook inside the fish. This is more easily accomplished when the hook

## TED WILLIAMS ON CATCH-AND-RELEASE FISHING

Ted Williams was a famous Red Sox player, a noted pilot for the U.S. Marine Corp during World War II, and a proficient fisherman. He fished all over the United States, and he particularly liked fly fishing. During his many years of fishing, he noticed fewer and fewer fish in the waters he fished regularly.

In a 1989 essay in *Popular Mechanics* magazine, Williams wrote about the need for catch-and-release fishing and other measures to protect the environment and fish populations. He was quoted as saying: "The first time you set a big one free feels kind of strange, maybe even a little painful. But the next one is easier and after that, they're all easy. You don't have to have a dead fish to prove you caught it. You know you did, and that's all that's important."

is in the throat and not all the way into the stomach. However, this will obviously greatly reduce the fish's chances of survival. This is especially true for saltwater fish like striped bass because the hook can rust in the salt water.

Working quickly when removing a hook from a fish is important, but it's equally important to work carefully. Try not to do more damage to the fish. It's easy for a hook still attached to a wriggling fish to become caught on a piece of clothing, a hand, or a finger.

Try to keep the fish in the water as you remove the hook. This isn't always possible due to the fish's motions and the weather or water conditions. Try to gently pick the fish up while wearing damp cotton gloves. Or, put a damp towel or cloth over the fish's head or body to handle it. Wearing damp gloves or using a towel does less damage to the mucus coating that protects the fish from becoming ill. Keep a gentle but firm hold on the fish. Don't let the fish flop around on the ground or the bottom of the boat, which can also cause a lot of damage to the fish. It also makes it more likely that the hook can become more lodged in the fish or even caught on a person.

Once the hook is removed, the fish can be released. If the fish is already in the water, simply let go of the fish and it will swim away. Never throw or toss the fish back in the water. Rather, gently place it in the water. If the fish is not moving much, it may be stressed. If this is the case, hold it upright in the water as gently as you can. Moving the fish forward will allow water to flow through its gills and help revive it. If the fish is in a river, let the fish go with the current, not against it. Once the fish begins to move on its own, release it into the water.

The longer a bass is in the water, the greater the chance that it will survive once you release it.

## STAYING SAFE AROUND WATER

Because fishing takes place in and around all kinds of bodies of water, all anglers need to learn good water safety practices. Perhaps the most important rule of water safety is to always wear a PFD, especially when you are in a fishing boat or at a dock. It's not enough to store a PFD on the boat or in a nearby container. It can be too difficult, and sometimes too late, to put one on if a boat capsizes. Even good swimmers should always wear a PFD. When buying a PFD, make sure it fits snugly but not too tightly.

Fishers should know how to swim before heading out on any fishing trip. Many schools and local recreation programs offer swimming lessons. If possible, take water safety classes at school, a local Red Cross, or another program. Water safety classes can teach procedures for how to help someone who has fallen overboard or how to flip an overturned canoe.

You should also be familiar with the body of water before venturing out on a fishing trip. This is especially important in deeper rivers with a fast-moving current. Be aware of the current and how strong it is. Sometimes, the surface of a river or stream looks calm but underneath, the water is moving quickly. Be careful to avoid dangerous objects such as logs or branches floating downstream. Avoid rocky areas and rivers that have rapids.

It's also important to be alert when fishing at the ocean shore. In some locations, the tide can come in or out quickly, particularly near rivers that flow into the ocean. When this happens, water can rise or lower swiftly, leaving anglers in unsafe conditions. Waves can take fishers by surprise if they aren't being careful.

The bottoms of many bodies of water are often slippery, so take care when walking. Take small steps, and plant your feet firmly before taking the next step. Try to put your feet between rocks rather than on top of rocks because rocks can be covered with algae or other slippery material. You can use a stick or tree branch to find the bottom of a lake or creek. You should always find out how deep a body of water is before fishing.

Boating safety is another important part of being safe around water. Don't overload a boat with people or equipment, which could make it hard or dangerous to move around. Make sure there's safety equipment on board, including a first-aid kit, lights, a horn, and PFDs for everyone on the boat. When navigating, be alert for other boats, obstacles, dams, rocks, waterfalls, and sandbars. Knowing an area well before taking a boat trip is a good idea. Also watch the weather conditions. Strong winds, high waves, and thunderstorms can be dangerous for any size boat. In some ocean locations, waterspouts can also be a hazard when fishing.

Some people don't mind fishing on a rainy or snowy day. However, you need to get away from water as quickly and safely as possible when a thunderstorm is in the forecast for your area.

Always watch out for thunderstorms, especially during the summer months. Check the forecast before heading out for a day of angling. If thunderstorms are in the forecast, consider changing the day or time of the trip. Even when a thunderstorm is not in the forecast, keep an eye on the skies for incoming clouds or rain. It's a good idea to monitor radios or smartphones to get updates on the forecast while angling.

Do not delay if you hear thunder: Take shelter immediately. A building or a car are the best choices. If neither is available, find the lowest place you can and stay near the smallest trees. If you are in a field, stand in an open area, away from tall trees, telephone poles, or metal fences. Take off anything made of metal.

A warning sign that a lightning strike is imminent is when the hair on a person's arms or head stands on end. If this happens, kneeling with your hands on knees and bent forward is the best position. This gives lightning the least amount of contact with the ground.

## FISHING GEAR SAFETY

Fishing gear can be dangerous when fishers don't follow appropriate safety measures. Some fishing equipment is sharp, so be safe and alert when working with hooks and knives. Only use a knife with clean, dry hands to avoid slipping. Wear gloves for extra protection. Be alert when using a knife, especially in a boat that can move suddenly. Also be alert when someone else is using a knife to avoid coming into contact with the knife by accident.

Barbless hooks are better for fish and also for the angler because they are less sharp. When a fishing pole isn't in use, always secure a hook on the line guide of the pole and make sure the line is tight. Or, better yet, remove the hook from the line when the pole isn't in use.

When handling fish, avoid touching their fins, which can be sharp. Gills can also be sharp. Some fish have spikes. Wearing cotton gloves when handling live fish, as mentioned previously, protects the fish. But even dead fish should be handled with gloves to avoid cuts, scrapes, and pokes.

## FISHING LAWS

Become familiar with local fishing laws and regulations before you even leave the house. It's the responsibility of the angler to know which fish are permissible to catch and if there are size or amount limits on those fish. Anglers must also know if a license is required for fishing.

Some states set length limits. For example, a law might require that any fish under 6 inches (15 cm) in length be released.

In some states, it's illegal to catch some types of fish. This is usually to protect rare or endangered types of fish. If caught, those fish must be released immediately and in good condition. Limits are often set to protect fish with a low population in a particular area.

Many states limit the number of fish of a certain type that can be caught by a fisher in one day. Other laws might apply to when fish can be caught. There are seasons when some fish shouldn't be caught. This does not apply to most types of bass, except striped bass in some cases. For example, in Maryland, it is illegal to fish for striped bass in areas where they spawn between March 1 and May 31.

You will need to pay a fee when getting a fishing license. Each state has its own fishing license, and anglers

# Attention Anglers

| | Daily Limit | Length Limit |
|---|---|---|
| Largemouth bass | 6 | 15" minimum |
| Crappie | 30 | none |
| Channel Catfish | 10 | none |
| Blue Catfish | 5 | none |
| Flathead Catfish | 5 | none |
| Walleye | 4 | 15" minimum |
| Warmouth | 15 | 7" minimum |
| White bass, striped bass, striped bass hybrids combined | 15 | No more than 4 over 18" |
| Common Carp | no limit | none |
| All other fish | statewide, up to 50 in the aggregate | none |

▲ **Pole and line fishing only (max. 3 poles/person),** except gizzard shad may be taken by dip net or throw net.

▲ Jackson County boating permit required for boating regulations.

▲ **Missouri Conservation Department**

*SPORT FISH RESTORATION*

Local authorities often provide public locations for fishing, but you will likely need to follow a lot of rules. Local regulations specify when fish can be caught, how many—if any—can be kept, and how long the fish must be.

must be licensed in the state where they want to fish. Most states offer annual licenses with different rates for state residents and non-residents. Some states issue different permits for saltwater and freshwater angling. There are sometimes reduced license prices for children and teens if the state does require a license. Licenses are good only for a certain length of time. Some states issue licenses that are valid for one season or for one full year. Others issue licenses for one calendar year.

Fishing licenses or permits can be purchased from local department of fisheries and wildlife offices. Most states also allow anglers to buy their licenses online. Fishing licenses help fund conservation and other state efforts to protect fish and enforce rules.

# CHAPTER 4

# AFTER THE CATCH

**M**any bass fishers use catch-and-release practices because they love the sport of fishing but don't want to kill the fish. However, in many cases, fishers choose to keep their catch to eat if it's permitted by local fishing regulations. Always check with local sources to make sure it's safe to eat fish caught in a particular body of water.

Read on to learn more about storing, preparing, and cooking the bass you've just caught!

## BASS ON ICE

If you plan to prepare a bass for eating, the priority is keeping it cool until it can be cleaned and cooked. Store the fish on ice as soon as possible after it's caught. The best way to keep fish fresh is in a cooler with ice and a bit of water. This will keep the fish cool and moist.

It's best to clean and fillet bass as soon as possible after catching them. If that's not possible, storing them on ice will keep them fresh until you can.

## FISH FILLETING

If you plan to cook your catch, clean the fish as soon as possible. Many docks and marinas have a designated fish-cleaning station. These stations will have water and facilities to throw out guts, scales, skin, and bones. These fish parts smell and attract flies and other insects, so they must be stored and disposed of quickly. Never clean a fish on a beach, dock, or other public area. If there's no place to clean your fish, keep it on ice until you get home. When cleaning fish at home, make sure to dispose of the discarded parts quickly. Wrap them well in plastic bags that can be sealed or knotted, and put them in tight, outdoor garbage cans. Use garbage cans with tight lids. If you neglect this step, you might attract unwanted wild animals, such as raccoons, bears, or coyotes.

Slicing a fish into thin portions for eating is called filleting. Filleting separates the skin and bones of a fish from its flesh. It's not an easy thing to do, but with some practice, it gets easier. However, it's best to have help from an adult or another experienced person for the first few attempts at filleting a bass.

A knife made for filleting fish is long and narrow. This helps the cook to cut neat fish fillets and remove tiny bones. Filleting knives need to be sharp so they slide through the fish flesh without much effort. If the fish flesh tears, the knife might not be sharp enough. Wear a pair of gloves for protection from sharp parts of the fish and from the knife. Fish tend to be slippery, so wearing gloves will provide a firmer grip.

A filleting knife can make cleaning and filleting a fish much easier. Remember that it's best to wear gloves when preparing a fish.

## TROPHY FISH

Some people like a souvenir to remind them of a particularly successful fishing trip. A process called taxidermy preserves a fish and mounts it so that it can be displayed. Back when fewer people practiced catch-and-release fishing, stuffing and mounting fish was more common.

Today, skilled artists can create replicas of fish that look like the real thing. To create an exact replica, the artist needs to know some basic information about the original fish. This includes weight, length, and coloring. Take a picture of the catch and take measurements before releasing it. This should give a taxidermist or artist enough information to create a trophy to hang on your wall.

Filleting a fish takes some practice, but it's not too hard once you practice. When filleting, start where the head meets the body. Begin cutting about 1 inch (2.5 cm) deep along the back to reach the backbone. Pull the flesh away from the ribs toward the stomach. Then cut the skin of the stomach down toward the tail, leaving the tail on. Turn the fish over and hold the tail. Working from tail to head, slide the knife between the skin and the meat of the fish. Do not force the knife. Let the sharp blade do the work. Repeat this process on the other side of the fish.

## CAREFUL COOKING

Bass is a healthy food. It's low in fat, and it's an excellent source of omega-3 fatty acids, which reduces the chances of heart disease. When it comes to eating bass, some kinds might be tastier than others. Largemouth bass have solid meat with a very fishy flavor. Many people prefer smallmouth bass for dinner. Its flesh is more tender and less fishy. Some describe it as sweet. Perhaps the most popular bass for eating is sea bass. Its flesh is sweet and mild flavored.

When deciding whether to eat a fish, keep in mind that it's best not to eat too many fish from the same area. Some waters contain contaminants that can become stored in a fish's body. These contaminants, especially mercury and chemicals known as PCBs, can be harmful to humans. You can contact state or local environmental offices to ask about local bodies of water and safe amounts of fish to eat from them.

Bass are not too fatty, but it's still a good idea to get rid of as much fat as possible. This is because contaminants are stored in the fatty parts of fish. Grilling or broiling bass will help burn off fat. Special grilling baskets or pans can make grilling fish easier. Fresh fish tastes so good that it's usually only necessary to cook it with a little olive oil or butter and some salt and pepper. Other flavors that go well with bass include lemon, garlic, dill, and onion.

# PAN FRIED BASS WITH LEMON GARLIC BUTTER SAUCE

## INGREDIENTS

· 4 largemouth bass fillets, skin removed
· salt
· pepper
· 1 cup (125 g) flour
· 4 tablespoons (60 ml) unsalted butter
· 1 tablespoon (15 ml) garlic, sliced thin
· mild fresh herbs such as basil, parsley, and oregano
· 2 tablespoons (30 ml) fresh lemon juice

## DIRECTIONS

1. Season the fillets with salt and pepper.
2. Heat a pan on top of the stove or grill. When the pan is hot, add the olive oil and allow it to heat up.
3. Drag the bass fillets through the flour and shake off any excess.
4. Place the fillets in the heated oil and fry for about 3 minutes per side, until golden brown. Remove the fish from the pan.
5. Add the butter to the pan. When the butter is melted, add the sliced garlic. Fry the garlic until it begins to turn light golden brown.
6. Add the herbs and remove from the heat.
7. Add the lemon juice.
8. Season with salt and pepper again.
9. Place a fillet on a plate and spoon some of the lemon garlic herb butter over the fish. Do the same with the other fillets.

# CHAPTER 5
# THINKING ABOUT THE ENVIRONMENT

Fishing is a great way to enjoy the peace and beauty of nature. It's also a great way to get exercise, hang out with people with similar interests, and learn new life skills. However, it's the responsibility of every angler to fish responsibly and keep the environment clean. If we don't protect the natural environment and fish stocks, there may be many fewer fish to enjoy in the future.

Declining fish populations and contamination are two major problems that should concern every angler. They are serious problems, but they do have solutions.

## FISH POPULATIONS

In some areas, fish populations are in decline due to over-fishing and water pollution. Some of this is caused by agricultural processes and fertilizer runoff. We are capable of preventing pollution, but changes need to be made. It's important for every angler to help prevent these problems and be a part of the solution.

Many bodies of water around the United States and the world are polluted and in need of cleanup.

Overfishing is a major factor in the decline of fish populations. When a type of fish is fished too much, there aren't enough fish left to reproduce and keep the population at a steady or increasing level. Commercial fishing can be particularly problematic, as some fishers quickly reduce the numbers of popular eating fish such as tuna, swordfish, and cod. However, even sport fish, such as bass, are in decline. Catch-and-release fishing is a key effort in the struggle to counteract overfishing. Take care of fish so that they can return to the water in healthy condition and continue to reproduce.

Pollution is the other major contributing factor to declining bass populations. Some chemicals that enter the water from businesses and farms can kill fish immediately. Other chemicals and pollution reduce the amount of oxygen

## FISH AND WILDLIFE OFFICERS

Becoming a fish and wildlife officer can be an excellent career choice for people who love outdoor activities and the natural world. These professionals usually work for state or national organizations. They issue hunting, fishing, and boating licenses and enforce local and national laws. Fish and wildlife officers often interact with the public. Some may teach classes on hunting or fishing safety and rules, and some may demonstrate good conservation practices. Fish and wildlife officers also help to protect fish and other wildlife. They perform wildlife counts in a particular area to keep track of populations. They also rescue injured animals or capture animals that have entered populated areas. Some officers are trained to investigate criminal activities such as animal cruelty and poaching.

in the water. Over time, the oxygen level can become so low that fish are not able to survive.

The biggest way large amounts of contaminants enter bodies of water is through pollution from factories or manufacturing plants. Don't dump anything in bodies of water. When fishing, don't leave garbage or other pollutants behind that might end up in the water. Learn about local companies and potential pollutants that might harm the water and the plants and animals living in it. You can also write to local officials to encourage them to make stronger antipollution laws and regulations.

## MERCURY CONTAMINATION

Mercury is a naturally occurring chemical element that is commonly found in rocks in Earth's crust. It's most commonly found in the minerals cinnabar and metacinnabar. When these minerals are worn away by erosion and weather, mercury can end up in our water supplies. Dust with mercury can enter the air due to human activities, including burning coal, municipal waste, and medical waste. Mercury particles in the air are then washed into the water by rain.

Once in the water, mercury enters the bodies of fish and other marine organisms. Mercury remains in the organism's body, and if that animal is eaten, it enters the body of the animal that ate the contaminated organism. This means that fish (or other animals) that eat smaller organisms have higher mercury concentrations in their body. When humans eat these fish or animals, mercury contaminates our bodies as well.

Bass eat lots of smaller organisms. Because of this, they often contain high concentrations of mercury.

Largemouth, smallmouth, and striped bass are on the U.S. Environmental Protection Agency's (EPA) list of fish that should not be eaten by children and pregnant women. Teens and adults should only eat these types of fish occasionally. Frequently eating bass can result in mercury poisoning.

Always check with local officials to determine whether it's safe to eat fresh-caught fish.

Have you ever been bass fishing with your family or friends?
It can be a memorable adventure!

## WHAT CAN YOU DO?

If you're concerned about the environment and protecting wildlife, there are many things you can do to help. First, fish responsibly. Carefully follow all laws and regulations about where and when to fish. Remember that catch-and-release fishing helps protect fish populations for the future. Don't leave garbage behind in a fishing area and collect the garbage others may have left behind. When boating, be careful not to harm the natural environment. Avoid damaging marine plants with a boat's motor. Don't allow gas or oil to spill into the water.

You can also teach your friends and family about environmental problems and how they affect fish and fishing. You could start a club at school or in the community to promote safe fishing practices. You may even consider a career as a fish and wildlife officer and continue to spread good conservation practices in your professional career.

Fishing is an enjoyable and relaxing pastime for many people. By fishing responsibly, bass fishing can be a rewarding, lifelong activity.

# GLOSSARY

**angler** A person who fishes.

**brackish** Partly fresh, partly salt water.

**contaminant** A substance that adds impurities.

**current** Water moving continuously in a particular direction.

**fiberglass** A material made of glass particles fused together.

**graphite** A material made up of carbon fibers.

**hatchling** A small fish or animal recently hatched from an egg.

**humane** Showing sympathy or concern for others.

**irrigate** To supply with water by artificial means.

**lactic acid** An organic material that is created when carbohydrates are broken down in the body.

**mimic** To copy or imitate.

**monofilament** A single strand.

**mucus** A slick substance produced by the body to moisten and protect.

**navigational device** An instrument that aids in figuring out position, course, and distance traveled.

**nylon** A strong artificial substance.

**organism** A living person, plant, or animal.

**poach** To hunt animals illegally.

**predator** An animal that kills other fish or animals.

**reel** A device set on the handle of a fishing pole to wind up or let out the fishing line.

**replica** A close or exact copy.

**souvenir** Something that serves as a reminder.

**taxidermist** Someone who prepares and mounts the skins of animals or fish.

**troll** To drag a lure or bait through the water to mimic the movement of prey to attract fish.

Bourne, Wade. *Basic Fishing: A Beginner's Guide.* New York, NY: Skyhorse, 2015.

Cermele, Joe. *The Total Fishing Manual: 318 Essential Fishing Skills.* San Francisco, CA: Weldon Owen, 2017.

Hemingway, Ernest. *The Old Man and the Sea.* New York, NY: Scribner, 1995.

Jacobs, Tim. *Tactics for Bass and Other Warmwater Species.* Lanham, MD: Stackpole Books, 2023.

Kinnison, Joe. *Next-Level Bass Fishing: Innovative Techniques That Have Elevated the World's Best Anglers to the Top.* New York, NY: Skyhorse, 2021.

McCoy, Matthew. *Knot Tying for Beginners: An Illustrated Guide to Tying the 25 Most Useful Types of Fishing Knots.* Independently Published, TangledTales Books, 2022.

Schwipps, Greg. *Fishing for Dummies.* Hoboken, NJ: John Wiley & Sons, 2020.

Waiters, Lawrence. *How to Catch Large Mouth Bass for the Weekend Fisherman.* Independently Published, 2021.

# FOR MORE INFORMATION

## Association of Fish and Wildlife Agencies
1100 First Street, NE Suite 825
Washington, D.C. 20002
(202) 838-3474
email: info@fishwildlife.org
website: www.fishwildlife.org
Twitter: @fishwildlife
Facebook: /FishWildlifeAgencies
The AFW represents North America's fish and wildlife agencies and promotes management and conservation of fish and wildlife.

## Bass Federation Junior Anglers
2300 East Coleman Road
Ponca City, OK 74604
(580) 765.9031
website: bassfederation.com/tbf-youth/tbf-junior-anglers
The Junior Anglers program of the Bass Federation allows anglers aged 11 to 18 to be part of local bass-fishing clubs.

## Canadian Sportfishing Industry Association (CSIA)
171 Rink Street, Suite 102
Peterborough, ON K9J 2J6
(705) 745-8433
website: www.csia.ca
The CSIA works to preserve fishing opportunities for Canada's residents and visitors. This is accomplished through education and management.

**FishAmerica Foundation**
1001 North Fairfax Street Suite 501
Alexandria, VA 22314
(703) 519-9691
website: fishamerica.org
FishAmerica is working to preserve sportfish
populations and keep waters healthy in the
United States and Canada.

**The International Game Fish Association
(IGFA)**
300 Gulf Stream Way
Dania Beach, FL 33004
(954) 927-2628
email: hq@igfa.org
website: igfa.org
Facebook and Twitter: @TheIGFA
The IGFA is a nonprofit organization committed to
the conservation of game fish and the promotion
of responsible, ethical angling practices through
science, education, rule making, record keeping, and
recognition of outstanding accomplishments in the
field of angling.

**National Bass Anglers Association
(NBAA Bass)**
5998 N. Pleasant View Rd
Ponca City, OK 74601
(580) 765-2319
website: www.nbaa-bass.com
Facebook and Twitter: @nbaabass
NBAA Bass sponsors bass fishing tournaments and
provides resources for finding local bass fishing clubs.

# INDEX

# ABOUT THE AUTHOR

Dwayne Hicks has written books for kids and teens for over 10 years. He has been on numerous family fishing trips with his father and grandfather—they particularly enjoy fly fishing. Hicks lives in Buffalo with his two dogs and an aquarium full of fish.

# ABOUT THE CONSULTANT

Contributor Benjamin Cowan has more than 20 years of both fresh and saltwater angling experience. In addition to being an avid outdoorsman, Cowan is also a member of many conservation organizations.

# PHOTO CREDITS

Cover FtLaud/Shutterstock.com; pp. 4-5 Kichigin/Shutterstock.com; pp. 5, 36 FedBul/Shutterstock.com; pp. 6-7 Slawomir Kruz/Shutterstock.com; p. 9 Katelyn Redfin/Shutterstock.com; p. 10 Jessica Stroup/Shutterstock.com; p. 11 Steve Oehlenschlager/Shutterstock.com; pp. 13, 17 slowmotiongli/Shutterstock.com; p. 14 Nomad_Soul/Shutterstock.com; p. 16 RLS Photo/Shutterstock.com; p. 19 domnitsky/Shutterstock.com; p. 22 Fabien Monteil/Shutterstock.com; pp. 24-25 Tamakhin Mykhailo/Shutterstock.com; p. 27 (left) Trofimov Pavel/Shutterstock.com; p. 27 (right) Policarpio de Leon/Shutterstock.com; p. 28 Kuznetcov_Konstantin/Shutterstock.com; p. 31 ARENA Creative/Shutterstock.com; p. 34 goodluz/Shutterstock.com; pp. 38-39 Fleury9816/Shutterstock.com; p. 40 Edgar Lee Espe/Shutterstock.com; p. 43 txking/Shutterstock.com; p. 44 Kwanza Henderson/Shutterstock.com; p. 47 Ryno Botha/Shutterstock.com; p. 48 Steve Brigman/Shutterstock.com; p. 51 CLP Media/Shutterstock.com; p. 53 Bryan Forsyth/Shutterstock.com; p. 56 Jon Kraft/Shutterstock.com; pp. 58-59 Maclane Parker/Shutterstock.com; p. 60 gracious_tiger/Shutterstock.com; p. 62 (top) photocrew1/Shutterstock.com; p. 62 (bottom) Jeffrey B. Banke/Shutterstock.com; pp. 66-67 Roka/Shutterstock.com; p. 68 Teresa Otto/Shutterstock.com; p. 71 Freebird7977/Shutterstock.com; p. 72 sirtravelalot/Shutterstock.com.